BASKETBALL LEGENDS

Kareem Abdul-Jabbar
Charles Barkley
Larry Bird
Kobe Bryant
Wilt Chamberlain
Clyde Drexler
Julius Erving
Patrick Ewing
Kevin Garnett
Anfernee Hardaway
Tim Hardaway
The Head Coaches
Grant Hill
Juwan Howard
Allen Iverson
Magic Johnson
Michael Jordan
Shawn Kemp
Jason Kidd
Reggie Miller
Alonzo Mourning
Hakeem Olajuwon
Shaquille O'Neal
Gary Payton
Scottie Pippen
David Robinson
Dennis Rodman
John Stockton
Keith Van Horn
Antoine Walker
Chris Webber

CHELSEA HOUSE PUBLISHERS

SCOTTIE PIPPEN

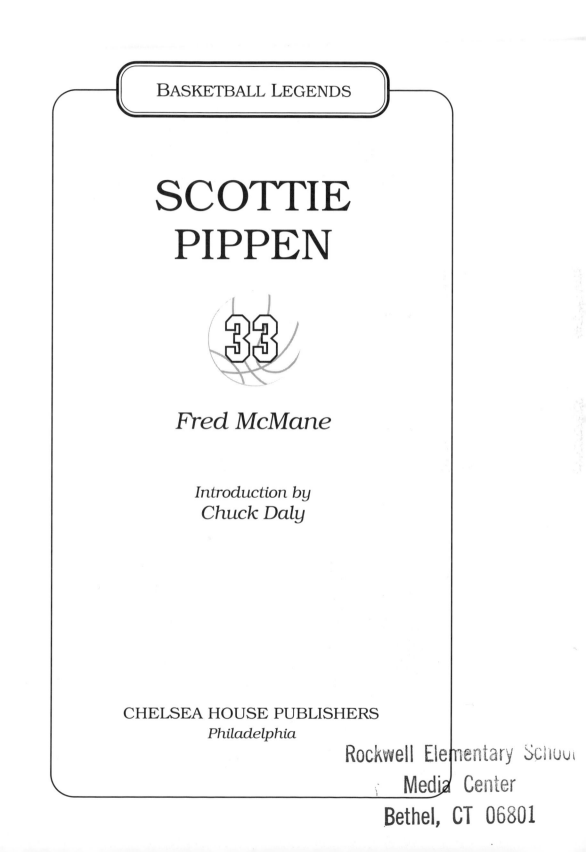

33

Fred McMane

Introduction by
Chuck Daly

CHELSEA HOUSE PUBLISHERS
Philadelphia

Produced by Daniel Bial and Associates
New York, New York

Picture research by Matt Dudley
Cover illustration by Bradford Brown

The Chelsea House World Wide Web address is
http://www.chelseahouse.com

7 9 8 6

Library of Congress Cataloging-in-Publication Data

McMane, Fred.
        Scottie Pippen / Fred McMane.
        p. cm. — (Basketball legends)
        Includes bibliographical references and index.
        ISBN 0-7910-2498-9
        1. Pippen, Scottie —Juvenile literature. 2. Basketball players—
United States—Biography—Juvenile literature. [1. Pippen,
Scottie. 2. Basketball players. 3. Afro-Americans—Biography]
I. Title. II. Series.
GV884.P55M36 1996
796.323'092—dc20
                                                    [B]95-18518
                                                        CIP
                                                         AC

CONTENTS

BECOMING A
BASKETBALL LEGEND

Chuck Daly

What does it take to be a basketball superstar? Two of the three things it takes are easy to spot. Any great athlete must have excellent skills and tremendous dedication. The third quality needed is much harder to define, or even put in words. Others call it leadership or desire to win, but I'm not sure that explains it fully. This third quality relates to the athlete's thinking process, a certain mentality and work ethic. One can coach athletic skills, and while few superstars need outside influence to help keep them dedicated, it is possible for a coach to offer some well-time words in order to keep that athlete fully motivated. But a coach can do no more than appeal to a player's will to win; how much that player is then capable of ensuring victory is up to his own internal workings.

In recent times, we have been fortunate to have seen some of the best to play the game. Larry Bird, Magic Johnson, and Michael Jordan had all three components of superstardom in full measure. The brought their teams to numerous championships, and made the players around them better. (They also made their coaches look smart.)

I myself coached a player who belongs in that class, Isiah Thomas, who helped leader the Detroit Pistons to two consecutive NBA crowns. Isiah is not tall—he's just over six feet—but he could do whatever he wanted with the ball. And what he wanted to do most was lead and win.

All the players I mentioned above and those whom this series will chronicle are tremendously gifted athletes, but for the most part, you can't play professional basketball at all unless you have excellent skills. And few players get to stay on their team unless they are willing to dedicate themselves to improving their talents even more, learning about their opponents, and finding a way to join with their teammates and win.

It's that third element that separates the good player from the superstar, the memorable players from the legends of the game. Superstars know when to take over the game. If the situation calls for a defensive stop, the superstars stand up and do it. If the situation calls for a big shot, they want the ball. They don't want the ball simply because of their own glory or ego. Instead they know—and their teammates know—that they are the ones who can deliver, regardless of the pressure.

The words "legend" and "superstar" are often tossed around without real meaning. Taking a hard look at some of those who truly can be classified as "legends" can provide insight into the things that brought them to that level. All of them developed their legacy over numerous seasons of play, even if certain games will always stand out in the memories of those who saw them. Those games typically featured amazing feats of all-around play. No matter how great the fans thought the superstars, the players were capable yet of surprising them, their opponents, and occasionally even themselves. The desire to win took over, and with their dedication and athletic skills already in place, they were capable of the most astonishing achievements.

CHUCK DALY, most recently the head coach of the New Jersey Nets, guided the Detroit Pistons to two straight NBA championships, in 1989 and 1990. He earned a gold medal as coach of the 1992 U.S. Olympic basketball team—the so-called "Dream Team"—and was inducted into the Pro Basketball Hall of Fame in 1994.

1

THE DEFINING MOMENT

Michael Jordan was way off his game. The strain of a league inquiry into his gambling habits and the pressure of trying to lead the Chicago Bulls to a third straight National Basketball Association (NBA) title had tired him out. He was in a dreadful shooting slump. The greatest basketball player who ever lived was missing shots that he usually made routinely.

It was Game 3 of the 1994 Eastern Conference finals and the Chicago Bulls, the two-time defending NBA champions, desperately needed a victory. The Knicks had won the first two games in New York and were in position to take a commanding 3-0 lead in the best-of-seven series.

The Bulls had entered the game in an angry mood. They had not talked to the news media in three days because they were dismayed at the questioning of a trip Jordan made to Atlantic City, NJ, where gambling is legal, after a Game 1 loss.

When Scottie Pippen dunked over John Starks in the 1993 playoffs, suddenly the Chicago Bulls had a new leader on the court.

The fans at Chicago Stadium were waiting for Jordan to take charge of the playoffs. Michael, though, was not up to the task on this day. He couldn't drop a pea into the ocean. The Bulls clearly needed someone else to step forward and take charge.

Their prayers would be answered by an unlikely hero—Scottie Pippen.

It was not that Pippen lacked talent to be a take-charge guy. He was one of the best players in the league. He had been an All-Star and a member of the "Dream Team" that won the gold medal at the 1992 Barcelona Olympics. He was considered among the top five best defensive players in the National Basketball Association.

But many basketball observers questioned whether Scottie had the strength of character necessary to be a team leader. He had developed a reputation for being "soft" in times of pressure during important games. The bad rap had started five years earlier when Scottie sat out the last quarter of the decisive Game 6 with Detroit after taking an elbow in the head from Pistons' center Bill Laimbeer. A year later his reputation as a quitter became even more widespread when he sat out Game 7 of the Eastern Conference final against Detroit with a migraine headache.

Despite his past reputation Scottie insisted he had the courage necessary to perform in the clutch.

"I know I'm not soft," Pippen said on the eve of the big series with the Knicks. "I know the type of player I am. I can't let what the public or the media say affect me. I've just got to go about what I'm doing."

Still, the Knicks' game plan for the series was to intimidate Pippen physically as much as was allowable under the rules. They knew those tactics would have little effect on Jordan. But they felt hard body contact would throw Pippen off his game.

New York and Chicago had squared off in the Eastern Conference final the previous year. Although the Knicks lost, their plan of intimidating Pippen had worked well. Forward Xavier McDaniel had shut him down almost completely. Pippen had played that series with a sprained ankle and was unable to shake the relentless pursuit of McDaniel.

The Knicks believed they could get the same kind of defensive pressure from Charles Oakley, Anthony Mason, and Charles Smith this time around. The strategy worked in the first two games, won by the Knicks, as Pippen was a nonfactor.

The crowd also got on Pippen, as fans in Madison Square Garden chanted "Charmin, Charmin" (after the "squeezably soft" bathroom tissue), whenever he touched the ball.

Also, if Jordan was not up to par, whoever would direct the team would need a cool head. Scottie had not displayed self-control near the end of Game 2 when he tossed the ball to referee Bill Oakes after being called for a double

Charles Smith of the Knicks could not find his shot against the combined defense of Scottie Pippen and Horace Grant.

dribble. Oakes immediately kicked Pippen out of the game, claiming that Pippen had not flipped him the ball but thrown it at him in anger.

"I did not double. I felt like it was a bad call," Pippen said in his defense. "I think the fans forced him to make the call and not only that but the fans made him eject me from the game. There was no reason I should have been ejected from the game.

"I felt like they tried to make him think I tried to embarrass him. I did not try to do that, no way."

Certainly there was nothing in Scottie's childhood to suggest that he could be a team leader. The youngest of 12 children from a small town in rural Arkansas, he never showed signs of being more than an ordinary player as a youngster. It wasn't until his senior year of college that he unveiled exceptional skills.

In fact, Pippen had accepted his role as second fiddle to the great virtuoso Jordan with the Bulls. Even Jordan had questioned publicly if Pippen had the will necessary to be a great player. But now Jordan was floundering. Now was the time for the understudy to become a star.

Not only did Pippen steal the spotlight, he gave the fans a show-stopping number to boot.

Pippen's emergence onto center stage came in the second period of Game 3. He had the ball in full stride at midcourt and had only the Knicks' John Starks to beat for the basket. As he neared the basket, Pippen leaped high and unleashed a ferocious tomahawk dunk over Starks that sent the Knicks' guard sprawling to the court. The Chicago Stadium crowd went wild and as Pippen trotted back up court he gave Starks only a slight, unconcerned glance.

From that moment on, the game belonged to Scottie Pippen. While Jordan struggled through a 3 for 18 shooting performance, Pippen took 12 shots and made 10 of them. He also was 8 of 10 from the foul line for a game-high 29 points as the Bulls won, 103–83.

Jordan, in fact, was content to be the play-maker and gladly turned over the bulk of the scoring to Pippen. Jordan finished with 11 assists, most of them passes to Pippen and guards John Paxson (14 points) and B. J. Armstrong (11 points).

"Controversy can hurt a team," Pippen said following the victory. "In this case, I think it helped us. I thought we came out with a lot of energy. Our defensive effort was great and the fans gave us great support. We hit our shots today. When we're shooting that well and Pax and B. J. are knocking down those shots, we're hard to beat."

The Knicks would not win another game. The Bulls won the next three to clinch their third consecutive Eastern Conference title.

Although Jordan regained his touch to score 54 points in Game 4, Pippen took charge in Games 5 and 6.

In Game 5 he scored 28 points and blocked New York's Charles Smith's final two lay-up attempts in the final seconds. During the decisive Game 6, Pippen came through in the clutch repeatedly.

When the Knicks threatened to steal the last game in the fourth period, Pippen hit two straight jump shots with the 24-second clock almost at zero and bailed out the Bulls. The first came from the deep right corner and the second was a three-pointer from beyond the top of the

Pippen celebrates after hitting a three-point shot to oust the Knicks from the 1993 playoffs.

key. After the second one he raised his index finger into the air and glowered at Starks.

Pippen finished the game with 24 points, 7 assists, and 6 rebounds. After the game Bulls' coach Phil Jackson sang Pippen's praises.

"It's no secret," Jackson said. "So goes Scottie Pippen, so goes Chicago."

The Knicks' Doc Rivers paid Pippen the ultimate tribute. "I hope you all get off his back now," Rivers told the media. "To beat us you have to be tough, and he beat us."

One of the first questions Pippen was asked following the clinching victory was if he thought this was the series in which he proved himself.

Pippen took a deep breath then said softly, "I have two championship rings. I don't think I have anything to prove."

He would soon have three rings. The Bulls met the Phoenix Suns, champions of the Western Conference, in the NBA finals and Chicago won the best-of-seven series, four games to two. The Bulls became the first team to win three straight league titles since the Boston Celtics captured their eighth in a row in 1966.

Although Jordan regained his hero's role in the final series and captured his third straight Most Valuable Player award, Pippen had proven himself to be more than just a capable sidekick.

He had become a star attraction in his own right, awaiting the day when he might lead the Bulls into battle instead of Michael Jordan. That day would come sooner than he expected.

2

NOTHING SPECIAL

There's nobody back in Hamburg, Arkansas, who ever expected Scottie Pippen's day in the spotlight would come at all.

Tucked in the southeastern part of the state, Hamburg (pop. 3,400) is the kind of small, rural town from which few escape. Leaving the drudgery of a little town and making it on your own in the big city is rare. Very few ever achieve it. Oh, Scottie dreamed about it all right. Night and day his mind was filled with the fantasies that young boys harbor about sinking the winning shot in the final seconds of the seventh game of the NBA championship.

"I would be on the playground court daydreaming that I was Julius Erving," Scottie said. "It would be the last game of the championship series. I had the ball and I was taking the last shot of the game."

But, in reality, Scottie was not particularly good at basketball as a youngster. Nor was he very big. His chances of making it beyond the

In high school, Scottie was an average player at best.

Hamburg paper mill where his father worked were remote.

"He wasn't really a basketball player," his mother, Ethel, recalled. "I remember he got into baseball games. He was just a nice boy."

There were few sports stars from Hamburg for Scottie to emulate. Hamburg's most famous athlete was Myron Jackson, who had gone on to play basketball at the University of Arkansas in Little Rock and then had a tryout with the Dallas Mavericks in 1986.

But Scottie had one thing going for him that many other youngsters his age did not. He came from a close-knit family. He was the youngest of 12 children and wasn't teased or babied by any of his brothers or sisters.

"My sisters would have me do little things for them," Scottie said. "Do this, do that, a couple of dollars here or there. I was one of those kids who always wanted to have a couple of dollars in my pocket."

Scottie's father, Preston, worked long hours at the Georgia Pacific paper mill, but he always made time for his children. Strong parental love and guidance helped make Scottie into a caring and responsible person.

"Scottie was well liked by his peers and teachers," recalled one of Pippen's high school guidance counselors, Dorothy R. Higginbotham.

When Scottie was in the ninth grade, his father suffered a stroke that left him paralyzed in a wheelchair and unable to speak. It was a hard blow for the family. But everyone pitched in and contributed to the family's well-being.

Meanwhile, Scottie was still trying to find his identity through sports. He played football in junior high, but by the time he was a sophomore in high school he had grown to be 6'0", the same height as his mother. Although six feet is taller than the average full-grown male, it is considered small by basketball standards. Still, Scottie tried out for the varsity basketball team and made the club as a reserve. But he did not get to play in many games.

In Pippen's junior season he angered the basketball coach by skipping the team's preseason conditioning program to serve as the equipment manager for the football team.

"I love football," Scottie said. "It was never my sport to play, but I enjoy watching and I wanted to be around the game."

Donald Wayne, the varsity basketball coach, did not want to let Pippen back on the team. But he put it to a vote of the players and they agreed to let Scottie rejoin the team. Still, Scottie played little.

In his senior year, everything began to change for Pippen. Most of the varsity team had graduated and Scottie earned the starting point guard position. He had grown another inch to 6'1" and because he was so skinny he had polished his ballhandling skills.

He performed well for the varsity. The team won 20 games and went on to the regional of the state championships. Yet there had been nothing exceptional about Pippen's game—nothing flashy or even noteworthy to attract the attention of college scouts.

"Nobody saw any NBA potential in Scottie," said Coach Wayne. "He was nothing fancy. He just did what he had to do."

"He was a good basketball player, but not anything really great," recalled David Moyers, editor and owner of the *Ashley County Ledger*,

Scottie's favorite sport in high school was football. Although he's wearing the number 80 shirt here, he only served as the team's equipment manager.

who saw Pippen play in high school.

Even Scottie's mother saw nothing unusual about her son. No thoughts of his sinking the winning shot in Game 7 of the NBA finals ever crossed her mind.

"He was an average kid who didn't get into trouble," she said. "He never made you think he'd do anything special."

Even though Scottie performed well during his senior year there were no college recruiters knocking on his door. There seldom are when you stand 6'1" and weigh only 150 pounds.

He was given a tryout at South Arkansas University, but the coaching staff sent him home without a scholarship offer.

Coach Wayne knew that the only way Pippen would get an opportunity to go to college would be on a basketball scholarship, so he called an old friend, Don Dyer.

Dyer was the coach at the University of Central Arkansas in Conway. It was a small school that participated in the National Association of Intercollegiate Athletics (NAIA) instead of the more famed National Collegiate Athletic Association (NCAA).

Wayne told Dyer that he had a point guard for him. "He's only 6'1", but he may still be growing," Wayne told Dyer.

Dyer took a chance. He obtained a Basic

Education Opportunity Grant for Pippen and arranged for him to attend Central Arkansas on a work-study basis as the team manager. That meant that in addition to practicing with the team, Pippen was in charge of the team's equipment, including laundry.

Coach Wayne had been right, though. Scottie was still growing. When Scottie arrived at Central Arkansas he had grown two inches. Coach Dyer's gamble was about to pay off beyond his wildest dreams.

3

WALK-ON TO GLORY

Scottie did not arrive at the University of Central Arkansas with any great aspirations of becoming an NBA player.

That goal would come much later. In fact, when he arrived on campus he wasn't even sure he wanted to play varsity basketball. He was under no obligation to do so. His work-study program did not guarantee him any place on the varsity team. Like everything else, if he wanted to do that, he would have to work hard for it.

"I wasn't really that interested in playing," Scottie told *Sports Illustrated*. "I had gone through some hard times not playing in high school, but my coach had it in his mind that basketball was the way I would get an education."

Coach Dyer told Scottie that he might be able to make the team in a year or two if he worked out with weights to build up his upper body strength. But he got a chance to make the

When Scottie got a chance to make the team in college, he made the most of his opportunity.

The University of Central Arkansas Bears were not a very good team, but they allowed Pippen to develop all his talents. He played all five positions and led his team in scoring and rebounding for three years.

team sooner than expected when several members of the team quit. As a freshman, Scottie saw some action as a reserve and, although he averaged only 4.3 points per game, he impressed the coach with his hustle and desire.

By the time his sophomore year started in the fall of 1985, Pippen had grown to 6'5" and become a player of rare talent. Because of his expericncc as a playmaker in high school, he had the mentality and ballhandling skills of a point guard. Now he also possessed the height of a forward.

Pippen's unique talents enabled him to play all five positions, and he quickly developed into Coach Dyer's best player. He led the team in scoring (18.5 points per game) and rebounding (9.2 per game) in his sophomore year. And when the season was over, he began working out with weights.

Pippen got bigger and stronger. Not only was his body filling out but he began to get a sense of what he wanted to do with his life. An industrial-education major, Pippen had spent two summers working in furniture plants and hoped to find a job as a factory manager after getting his degree. But he was now beginning to think seriously about a career in professional basketball.

In Pippen's junior year, Coach Dyer asked all his players to fill out a card explaining what their goals were for the future. Scottie wrote on his card, "I would like to be an NBA player."

"It was the first time I'd ever said it," Scottie recalled. "Before that I would have been ashamed."

Scottie was the team's leading scorer (19.8 per game) and rebounder (9.2 per game) again in his junior year and was named to the NAIA All-America team.

Pippen became a dominant player in his senior season. He had grown to 6'7" and was still the team's point guard. No one could stop him. He averaged 23.6 points, 10.0 rebounds, and 4.3 assists per game. He connected on 59 percent of his field goal attempts, including 58 percent from three-point range. He was named an NAIA All-America selection for the second straight year.

It was beginning to look as if Pippen might be good enough to make the NBA, but he had another problem to overcome. Playing for Central Arkansas got him no exposure. The team failed to make the NAIA tournament finals in Kansas City during Pippen's career. The school had never sent a player to the NBA in its history.

It is difficult for players from small colleges to get noticed. The quality of competition is much stronger at the major NCAA Division 1A colleges. Pro recruiters have often seen stars at small colleges fold when they play against more competitive teams.

Marty Blake, the director of scouting for the NBA, came to see him play. He was impressed, and advised all the NBA teams to take a look at Pippen. But only Jerry Krause, the general manager of the Chicago Bulls and a former scout

Pippen soars to the hoop in a game against Ouachita Baptist College. The Bears' opponents were rarely more than mediocre, which led pro scouts to wonder how he would do against top-flight competition.

who took pride in finding talented players in obscure places, took Blake's advice.

Krause sent an assistant, Billy McKinney, to Conway to scout Pippen. McKinney was not impressed with the competition Central Arkansas faced that night. "Amateur night at the Y" was how he put it in his report to Krause. Still, McKinney was enamored of the large hands, long arms, and leaping ability of Pippen, who scored 29 points, grabbed 14 rebounds, and made 5 steals that night. These were qualities that Krause admired in a young prospect and he predicted that Pippen would be a high second-round pick in the NBA draft. Krause was eager to make Pippen the steal of the draft.

Not knowing of the Bulls' interest in drafting Scottie, Blake decided to showcase Pippen's talents for the NBA scouts. He invited Scottie to participate in a postseason all-star game in Portsmouth, Virginia.

There are several all-star games after the regular college season ends during which the top players from around the country play against each other. It is a good way for lesser-known players to show the scouts what they can do against the best college players in the country.

This game in Portsmouth attracted many of the NBA's top scouts and general managers, including Krause. Pippen had never played against the top players from high-profile schools, but he wasn't intimidated. He played so well that he was named to the all-tournament team.

Pippen's performance earned him an invitation to an even more prominent all-star game in Hawaii. This one featured many of the nation's

All-American selections. Pippen performed even better this time. He was named to the all-tournament team and won the dunking contest. Now every scout in the land was interested in him.

"The scouts didn't know who to call," remembered Pippen's agent, Jimmy Sexton. "No one from the network—Bobby Knight, Dean Smith—knew who he was."

One thing was certain. Jerry Krause was not going to be able to sneak Pippen through the draft. "We wanted to try to sneak him past people," said McKinney, "but you can't hide a guy with that kind of ability."

Krause was still determined to get Pippen in the draft, but he was certain that the Los Angeles Kings wanted him, too. So Krause, who had the number 7 pick, knew he would have to outmaneuver the Kings, who had the number 6 pick.

Krause called the Seattle SuperSonics, who had the number 5 pick, and asked them if they would be willing to work out a trade. Krause asked them to use their pick to draft Pippen, then trade him to Chicago.

The SuperSonics agreed to the switch if the Bulls would give them veteran forward Olden Polynice. The deal took hours to put together but at 4 a.m. on the day of the 1987 draft it was completed.

The Bulls signed Scottie to a six-year contract worth more than $5 million. Scottie immediately bought a new house for his parents. In four years he had advanced from passing out socks to being a player the Bulls were counting on to help take the pressure off their superstar, Michael Jordan.

A wondrous journey was about to begin for the quiet kid from Arkansas.

4
LIFE WITH MICHAEL

Scottie did not know what to expect when he joined the Bulls at training camp in the summer of 1987. The Bulls had the greatest player in the world in Michael Jordan but not much of a supporting cast to go with him. The team was searching for an identity as more than a group of chorus boys behind a lead singer.

Although Pippen had played mostly guard in college, Bulls' coach Doug Collins took one look at him and decided to use him as a backup small forward behind starter Brad Sellers.

Scottie's performance in his first season was for the most part ordinary. He averaged 7.9 points per game while connecting on 46.2 percent of his field goal attempts and just 57.6 percent of his free throws.

Still, there were times when he displayed great athleticism. Pippen showed abilities as a passer and ballhandler that were better than many of the league's point guards. His quick-

Pippen's athleticism made him a natural complement to Michael Jordan (left).

ness and jumping ability were comparable to Jordan's. Because of his long arms he was a standout defensive player and solid rebounder, especially on the offensive boards.

The Bulls won 50 games during the regular season but were eliminated in the second round of the playoffs by the Detroit Pistons, four games to one.

Chicago fans, though, were excited. For the first time since Jordan joined the club, the future looked bright. Pippen had shown that with more experience he might be one of the top players in the league and could prove to be the buffer needed to take the pressure off Jordan.

Scottie was eager for the 1988 training camp to begin, but he got off to a bad start when it was discovered that he needed surgery to repair a herniated disk in his back. The surgery forced him to miss the entire preseason, and he also sat out the first eight games of the regular season.

When he finally returned to the lineup he continued to substitute for Sellers for the first 16 games. But on December 27—two days after Christmas—Scottie got the break he had been looking for. Collins named him as the starting small forward.

For the remainder of the season Scottie averaged 14.4 points, 6.1 rebounds and 3.5 assists per game.

In the first round of the Eastern Conference playoffs against the tough Cleveland Cavaliers, Scottie averaged 15 points and 8.6 rebounds per game as the Bulls won, three games to two.

The Bulls then beat the New York Knicks in the second round and advanced to the conference finals for a rematch with the Pistons. The series would prove to be a nightmare for Pippen and leave him with a stigma that he would not lose for five years.

The Pistons had earned a reputation as the "bad boys" of the NBA because of their physical, intimidating style of play. They were all over Pippen, bumping him on every possible occasion in an effort to break his concentration and take him out of his game. Their tactics worked; Pippen struggled.

Despite Scottie's problems, the Bulls took a 2–1 lead in the best-of-seven series. Detroit, though, came back to win the next two. In the first minute of play in Game 6, Pippen was elbowed in the head by center Bill Laimbeer. He suffered a concussion and did not return to the game. Detroit won the game and clinched the Conference title. The Pistons then swept the Los Angeles Lakers in four games to win the NBA title.

Pippen came under heavy criticism from the news media and the fans for not returning to the decisive sixth game. What they did not

In 1988, clutch baskets by Pippen helped the Bulls defeat the Cleveland Cavaliers in the playoffs. Here the rookie celebrates with teammate Mike Brown.

know, however, was that Pippen had wanted badly to go back in but was kept out of it by Bulls' general manager Jerry Krause on the advice of the team doctor.

"People later criticized Scottie," Krause told *Chicago* magazine in January 1994. "But he is a tougher kid than most people think. He begged me to let him go back into that game—he just begged me and begged me. But, in the end, I just had to go with the doctor's advice."

Laimbeer's elbow aside, it was clear that Pippen was emerging as one of the top players in the league. What he needed was more opportunities to show off his great skills. Collins' offense was too confining. Pippen needed a coach with a more creative approach.

Enter Phil Jackson.

Jackson, a wiry, broad-shouldered, studious type who had been a key contributor to a championship season with the New York Knicks 20 years earlier, was named Bulls' coach for the 1989–90 season. He and assistant Tex Winter immediately designed an offense geared to take advantage of both Jordan's and Pippen's unusual talents.

In order to develop a more balanced attack, the Bulls installed a triangle offense, a motion-oriented attack in which players without the ball moved to open spaces on the floor. The triangle created new opportunities for Pippen. He became a "point forward"—a combination of point guard and small forward. It would enable Pippen to be more creative on the open floor.

"I feel like I can be as good as I let myself be," Pippen said. "It's just a matter of working hard. I've worked to improve my defense and shooting off the dribble. I know I'm a better spotup shooter, but I'm trying to pull off the dribble when the lane is blocked."

Pippen blossomed in Jackson's new offense. He averaged 16.5 points per game but his defense was even more impressive. He had 211 steals, the third best total in the NBA, and he blocked 101 shots. His performance earned him a spot on the NBA All-Star team. Moreover, the Bulls finished the regular season in second place in the Central Division.

During the playoff series with the Philadelphia 76ers, Pippen's father died. Somehow he managed to play despite his heartache and the Bulls advanced to the Eastern Conference finals for another show-down with the Pistons.

It was clear from the outset of the series, however, that Pippen was not himself. He played poorly in Game 1 and in the first half of Game 2. His performance was so bad that Jordan had a lockerroom tantrum during halftime of Game 2, accusing several of the Bulls' players of not having the intestinal fortitude to win. He did not name names but it was clear that Pippen was included in his harangue.

Pippen was playing so badly that the Pistons decided to drop a defensive man off him and double up on Jordan.

One Chicago columnist wrote: "Hello, Missing Pippens Bureau, I mean, Missing Persons Bureau. I'd like to report a lost for-ward. An All-Star."

Despite Pippen's horrid play, the two teams battled each other evenly through six games. But during the warm-ups preceding the decisive seventh game, Scottie was stricken with a severe migraine headache.

Detroit's Bill Laimbeer throws an outlet pass after elbowing Pippen in the head. Detroit ousted Chicago from the playoffs in 1989 for the second straight year.

"It was like an ice pick was lodged in my skull," he recalled.

He decided to play anyway and was on the court for 42 minutes. But he made just 1 of 10 field goal attempts and finished with just 2 points and 4 rebounds. At one point during the first half, Pippen signaled to coach Jackson that he wanted to come out of the game. Scottie sat on the bench with a towel wrapped around his head and an ice bag on top of it.

The game was no contest as the Pistons romped to a 93–74 victory. Detroit then beat the Portland Trailblazers in five games to win its second straight NBA title.

Scottie thought he might be seriously ill and checked into a hospital a few days later to get a brain scan. When the test proved negative, Scottie was relieved. But the attacks on his personal courage from the media and fans bombarded him.

Sports journalists were especially vicious in

their attack on Pippen's character. For the second year in a row, he had not been at his best in the big game. The image of Pippen sitting on the bench with a towel draped over his head seemed to prove that in crunch time the Bulls remained a one-man team.

"It's something the fans will never let die," Scottie later admitted. "Then again, it's something I look over and I don't really think much about it. I think for us to win Michael and I have both got to play well. You can't beat good teams with just one player performing well. If you do, you're not going to beat them more than once."

Scottie knew, though, that the only way he would be able to shed his image as a "choker" was to help bring the Bulls an NBA title.

Somehow Pippen's failure in the 1990 playoffs and the death of his father helped him mature as he entered the 1990–91 season. He came to training camp in the best shape of his career. He had put on 10 pounds of muscle after working out all winter and now tipped the scales at 218.

"The things that have happened for me, to me, have helped me grow up," Pippen said. "Especially the passing of my father. That was something that took me to another level of growing and maturing. That's when I decided to be more of a man."

Pippen excelled during the preseason games but when the season started he found himself distracted by a bitter contract dispute with Bulls' management.

He created a controversy in February by skipping a practice, just one day after the Bulls had established the best record in the East. Pippen told the Bulls he was irked that management was slow in trying to sign him to a new contract. He pointed out that his $765,000-a-year salary made him only the sixth-highest-paid player on the team.

"I'll finish the season if I stay healthy, but my heart won't be in it," he said. "I can't guarantee what kind of effort they'll get out of me because I am really upset."

It was not until March that the squabble was resolved and Pippen received an extension that would pay him $3.5 million per year through the 1997–98 season.

Scottie emerged as one of the premier players in the league during the 1990–91 campaign. He averaged 17.8 points and posted a career best 52 percent field goal accuracy. He also grabbed 595 rebounds, registered 511 assists, and had 193 steals.

There were times, however, when Pippen had to endure the taunts of fans, who would not let him forget his performance in Game 7 of the previous season's playoffs.

In a meaningless season finale against the Pistons, Pippen missed a free throw in the third quarter and a Chicago fan stood and yelled, "Hey, Pippen, what's the matter? Got a migraine?"

The Bulls finished the regular season in first place in their division with a 61-21 record. They were 11 games ahead of their archrival, the Pistons.

During the first two rounds of the playoffs against the Knicks and Philadelphia 76ers, the Bulls lost only one game. It earned them another shot at the Pistons for the Eastern Conference title.

This time it was no contest. The Bulls swept

the Pistons in four games, with Scottie playing an integral role. Chicago had earned the right to meet the Lakers for the NBA title.

5

EASY AS ONE, TWO, THREE

Scottie's emergence as a superstar had placed the Bulls among the NBA's elite. General manager Jerry Krause had slowly built a club that had balance and depth. In addition to Jordan and Pippen, the team had a strong young forward in Horace Grant, a veteran center in Bill Cartwright and a sharpshooting guard in John Paxson. But they had to face a great team in the Los Angeles Lakers.

The Lakers featured Kareem Abdul-Jabbar at center, the all-time leading scorer in NBA history. Veteran All-Star James Worthy started at forward. A. C. Green was a great defensive player. The heart of the team was 6'9" guard Earvin "Magic" Johnson, an all-around phenomenon who had revolutionized the guard position. The Lakers had owned the Western Conference during the past decade, winning it every year except one between 1981–82 and 1988–89. Four times during the 1980s they won the NBA championship.

Chicago finally broke Detroit's domination in 1991. Here Pippen celebrates drawing a foul on Dennis Rodman.

Magic Johnson had his way against Chicago defenders in Game 1 of the 1991 championship series. Then Coach Jackson asked Scottie to guard Magic, and the Bulls won the next four games.

In 1991, the Lakers again had taken the Western Conference, and Magic Johnson was looking to keep up their winning ways. He was at his best in the opener and the Lakers won.

Coach Jackson knew he would have to make a change in his defensive alignment if the Bulls were to have a chance of winning. Jackson asked Pippen to guard Johnson.

Scottie accepted the formidable challenge and held Johnson in check for the rest of the series. The Bulls recovered from their embarassing defeat in the first game to win the next four and capture the franchise's first world championship. Scottie led all scorers with 32 points in the the decisive fifth game.

While the fans had snubbed Scottie by leaving him off the All-Star team, his defensive prowess earned him a spot on the second unit of the league's all-defensive squad. More importantly, any time his heart was questioned again by his critics he could point to his NBA championship ring as proof that he had conquered those demons.

Pippen was even better during the 1991–92 season. He raised his scoring average to 21 points per game and helped the Bulls win a league-best 67 games in the regular campaign. In addition, he was named to the NBA All-Star team.

The Bulls drew the Knicks in the first round of the playoffs and New York gave Chicago a difficult time. Scottie, in particular, was way off his game. He was playing on a sprained ankle and with a sore wrist. Thanks to Jordan, the Bulls won in seven games but once again Scottie's reputation as a poor performer in the clutch prevailed. He was bothered by his injuries and was pushed around repeatedly by Knicks' forward Xavier McDaniel.

Jordan again led the way as the Bulls defeated Cleveland for the Conference title then downed Portland in six games for their second straight NBA championship.

Critics hailed Jordan as the "greatest player who ever lived" but were less praiseworthy of Pippen, whom they labeled "too soft" to be considered among the NBA's top echelon of players.

Clearly, Scottie was going to have to prove himself all over again.

While the news media were harsh critics, NBA coaches were very respectful of Pippen's talents. Chuck Daly, coach of the Pistons, was one of his biggest boosters.

When Daly was named to coach the U.S. Olympic team in the 1992 Barcelona Games, he and his committee included Pippen on the list of probable selections for the team.

Donnie Walsh, general manager of the Indiana Pacers and a member of the Olympic selection committee, liked Pippen's flexibility: he could play small forward as well as both guard positions. San Antonio GM Bob Bass thought Pippen's style of play was perfectly suited for

European-style basketball, which were the rules under which the Olympic competition was conducted. He also was a fan of Pippen's defensive play.

When it came time to vote on who would comprise the Olympic team the general managers surprised many by selecting Scottie as one of the 12 members. Pippen was among a group of handpicked superstar players that also included Jordan, Magic Johnson, Larry Bird and Charles Barkley.

"I wasn't even sure I was one of the candidates," Pippen said upon learning that he had been one of Daly's original five choices. "All I knew was that, well, my day was coming."

Scottie was thrilled at the selection. "There's 27 teams and 12 players on a team. All these players are great and I'm one of the chosen few," he said. "It took me a long time to be that. The chosen few."

Making the Olympic team meant that he had been recognized as being more than Michael Jordan's caddie. It did wonders for Scottie's self-confidence.

The U.S. team steamrolled over its Olympic competition. The games were no contest. Scottie performed well, at times dazzling the fans with his high-flying moves to the basket. The experience of playing with the world's best players had raised his game to an even higher level.

Playing on the Olympic team had created a problem, however. There was not much time before the start of another NBA season. The Bulls' two superstars had little time to prepare for another grueling 82-game NBA campaign.

Few believed the Bulls could win a third straight championship. After all, how much could they expect to get out of Jordan and Pippen over a full season considering the amount of time they had put in with the Olympic team?

It turned out the Bulls got much more than they expected. Jordan led the league in scoring for the seventh straight season, averaging 32.6 points per game. Pippen's scoring average dipped some to 18.6 points per game, but he again started in the All-Star game and earned a spot on the league's defensive unit.

In late February, however, Scottie's streak of 300 consecutive games was broken when he was suspended for one game for throwing a punch at the Orlando Magic's Jeff Turner. Pippen argued unsuccessfully that he had merely slapped at Turner to make him let go of his shirt.

Pippen represented the United States in the Olympic Games. Here he drives down court as Israel Machado of Brazil and Patrick Ewing try to keep up.

The Bulls repeated as Central Division champions, but they had only the third best record in the league, behind New York and Phoenix. Chicago swept both the Atlanta Hawks and Cleveland Cavaliers in the early rounds, but the Knicks believed that without the home-court advantage the Bulls were vulnerable and could be denied a third straight title. Especially if they could intimidate Pippen.

The Knicks won the first two games in New York and their tough defense seemed to rattle

Michael Jordan holds the 1991 NBA Championship trophy, Bill Cartwright holds the 1992 trophy, and Scottie Pippen holds the 1993 trophy as the Bulls celebrate the first basketball threepeat since the mid-1960s.

both Jordan and Pippen. But when the series switched to Chicago, Pippen took charge. He led the Bulls to four straight victories as the Knicks were eliminated. Chicago then beat the Charles Barkley-led Phoenix Suns in six games to win a third consecutive championship.

Three in a row. No team since the Boston Celtics won eight in a row from 1959–66 had put together three straight championship seasons. Pippen had emerged as a team leader yet, more importantly, he had come to terms with playing in the shadow of the giant beacon that was Michael Jordan.

"I honestly don't know if I could function as a player away from Michael," Pippen told the *New York Times* during the 1993 playoffs. "What Michael has brought us, every night, every game, is the spotlight and the pressure that would have been directed elsewhere. All of us— Horace, Pax [John Paxson], B. J. [Armstrong]— had to respond to it, or else we would have died as a team. Eventually, we did respond and it made us stronger.

"I wanted more [recognition and shots] early in my career; sure, I did. It was hard always being compared to Michael because it seemed no one else was under the same microscope. You never heard about James Worthy being criticized because he didn't do enough to help Magic Johnson when the Lakers lost, for example. But with the Bulls, it was always, 'Well, Michael held up his end as usual, but Scottie didn't do enough.' I just came to realize that it was a unique situation with Michael because of how really great he is.

"It doesn't surprise me that teams come after me because they feel they can't get to Michael. I love that challenge. When I'm healthy there isn't a challenge in the world I can't meet.

"I've come to terms with my role on this team, and that is to do the things I can do. I'll never be the scorer Michael is. I couldn't put up those numbers even if I tried. And you know what? I hope he leads the league in scoring for the rest of his career. And when it's all over, I'll be able to say, 'I helped him do it. And I played with the greatest player ever.'"

Although he did not know it at the time, Pippen was about to find out just how well he could function without Jordan.

Before the start of the 1993–94 season, Jordan announced his retirement from basketball to pursue a career in baseball. After many years as the best basketball player in the world, Jordan had grown tired of the pace and sought to get away from the hustle and bustle of the NBA. Besides, the game was no longer challenging to him. He had accomplished everything he needed to accomplish.

Jordan's decision stunned the basketball world. Now the Bulls were Scottie Pippen's team. Everyone wondered if he had the maturity and wisdom to handle it.

6

ON HIS OWN

First it was Magic Johnson. Then Larry Bird. Now Michael Jordan. The three greatest superstars of the NBA's last 10 years had retired. Magic's team, the Los Angeles Lakers, and Bird's club, the Boston Celtics, had not recovered from the loss of their superstars.

Most expected the same fate to befall the Bulls. The consensus among basketball analysts was that without Jordan the Bulls would be lucky to make the playoffs. In the sports betting parlors of Las Vegas, the odds on the Bulls winning a fourth consecutive championship had been posted as 2–1 with Jordan playing. Without him, those odds had dropped to 25–1.

The load of carrying the team rested squarely on Scottie's shoulders.

"I'm not Michael Jordan," Pippen quickly retorted, "and I never could be. But I know that it is now up to me to provide some of the things that he provided. I tried to do that when he was

When Michael Jordan retired, Pippen had to explain to the media and Bulls fans how the team would fare.

playing and now [that he isn't] it is more important. . . ."

Even without Jordan, the Bulls had a formidable team. Horace Grant was among the league's best forwards and Bill Cartwright brought plenty of experience to the center position. B. J. Armstrong was a solid point guard and Stacey King, Scott Williams, and Will Perdue provided a solid bench.

There was even a newcomer who brought impressive credentials to the court. His name was Toni Kukoc, a native of Croatia who had played for the Croatian national team against the U.S. "Dream Team" in the Barcelona Olympics. Kukoc, a 6'11" guard, was the most celebrated player in Europe. The news media dubbed him "the European Magic Johnson" and he was a favorite of the Bulls management, who had hotly pursued him.

Pippen, who had been having problems with Bulls' management over his contract, did not immediately warm to Kukoc. Pippen was angry with the Bulls for spending so much money on a European player. Scottie, and others in the league, did not believe European players were as good as NBA players. After all, hadn't Pippen and Jordan combined to embarrass Kukoc and Croatia in the gold medal game at Barcelona?

As good as Kukoc was reported to be, however, he was still only a rookie and it would take time for him to adjust to the NBA. What the Bulls would miss most from Jordan—besides his points, defense and leadership—was his fearlessness and the fear he instilled in the opposition.

"I can't put on a bright face and say we'll be the same team," said John Paxson. "Michael Jordan defined who we are, and that's gone today."

Coach Phil Jackson agreed that Jordan's winning attitude—not to mention his 32 points per game—would be sorely missed. But he still believed the Bulls had enough talent to challenge again for the title. The club had made some key acquisitions before the season opened, adding Pete Myers, Bill Wennington, and Steve Kerr to the club.

"These ball players have been known as the Jordanaires the last three or four years," said Jackson. "This is a great opportunity for our team, for everyone, to step into areas in which we can suddenly establish ourselves.

"We think we can still compete at this level. One of the encouraging things that Michael said to us was, 'I wouldn't have retired if I didn't think you guys weren't ready to step up to the position where you can defend the championship.'"

When the Bulls opened the 1993–94 season team by losing seven of their first 12 games, the predictions of the analysts seemed right on target.

The Bulls, though, had been hit hard by injuries. Pippen missed 10 of the first 12 games with an ankle injury and Paxson and reserve center Scott Williams also were out with injuries. When Pippen returned in the 13th game of the season, the team's outlook brightened considerably.

The team won 14 of its next 15 games and, at the All-Star break, the club was tied for the best record in the conference. Pippen, Grant and Armstrong were elected to the All-Star team and Scottie used the opportunity to showcase his talents to an international television audience.

Wearing a brand new pair of red sneakers just to show "something different," Scottie scored 29 points, grabbed 11 rebounds, and added 4 steals to lead the East to a 127–118 victory over the West. He was an easy choice for Most Valuable Player.

"He was there the whole game," said East coach Lenny Wilkens. "He provided leadership throughout, he got out on the break, got the tough rebounds and played great support defense. He was head and tails above everybody else."

Pippen's leadership was shown best late in the game. He went to the bench for a rest with his team leading by 11. When the West cut the lead to one, Pippen reentered the game. He scored only one basket in the final 7:30 but had 2 steals, 3 rebounds, an assist and retrieved a crucial jump ball in the final minutes.

"I felt good," Scottie said. "This was an opportunity to come out and show myself. We (Bulls players) have been accused of riding Michael's coattails, but with B. J. and Horace in the All-Star Game and the way we've played as a team this season shows we've come out of his shadow."

The Bulls' performance in the first half of the season had been unexpected and now there was talk that they just might have enough to win a fourth straight title.

"What this team has done is proven to everyone that it was always very, very good," said Bulls assistant coach John Bach. "The real test will come in the playoffs. You have to be able to throw out bad days, play through adversity and find ways to win. Nobody did better than Michael. But if we can do it we'll make NBA history. The Lakers lost Magic Johnson and skidded. The Celtics lost Larry Bird and they've been floundering.

"New York will never be satisfied until they don't find the Bulls in front of them, just as we could never be satisfied until we rid ourselves of the Tasmanian Devils, the Detroit Pistons.

"Hopefully, New York won't find that way to beat us in the playoffs. I know their fans are looking forward to seeing us. But anyone who thought we wouldn't want to come to New York without Michael is in for a surprise. It's nice to fool people."

The truth was that while the Bulls were still very good, they were no longer dominant. When everyone was healthy, they were capable of beating anyone. But one injury to any key player could send them reeling.

Pippen and new Bulls star Toni Kukoc did not always see eye-to-eye.

Pippen and Kukoc were perfect examples of that. With Pippen out in the beginning of the season with his ankle injury, the Bulls were a sub-.500 team. Kukoc also missed some time with a strained lower back and the team floundered in his absence.

Indeed, Kukoc had become an integral part

*Off season, Pippen spends
a lot of time helping kids.*

of the team. His versatility, outside shooting, and passing skills blended in smoothly with the Bulls' system. Without Kukoc in the lineup, the Bulls lacked the size to move Pippen into the backcourt at will.

Yet, at times, Pippen made life difficult for Kukoc. He sometimes yelled at him on the court for failing to execute a play properly. As Kukoc became more comfortable with the NBA style of play, however, he became a valuable member of the team and Pippen softened in his criticism of the Croatian star.

"I think Toni is a very talented player," Pippen said. "He has a lot to learn about this game. . . .When he does emerge, it's going to be a sudden takeoff for him because he has so much talent. There are a lot of things this summer that he's going to have to take to another level if he's ever going to be a star.

"When I push Toni, I try to make him better, like Michael did me. People look at it wrong and assume I dislike him. The problems I supposedly had weren't personal. I objected to the way there were pursuing him and offering him so much money, and I was here helping us win championships and had to wait for a new contract. But that was business. It had nothing to do with Toni personally.

"I honestly enjoy talking to Toni and trying to teach him how to be a better player. I want us to have the same thing going Michael and I had. I see a lot of my game in Toni. He just needs somebody to push him every day."

Scottie had a bigger problem with general manager Jerry Krause. Not only was Pippen unhappy with his contract, but he was disappointed in Krause for not making a trade for a scorer to replace Jordan.

The Bulls were doing fine without Michael, but Scottie and the team knew for them to rcpcat as champions they needed another offensive force.

"We badly want to win four consecutive championships," Scottie told *Sport Magazine*. "We want him [Krause] to be fair to us, realizing that a team like New York is really trying to do all they can [to win a championship]. They lost Doc Rivers and replaced him within three weeks. We lost the greatest guy in the game and we never went out and tried to bring anybody in to really be a big threat.

"I mean, I like Pete Myers. He's been great for us in that (shooting guard) position. I don't think we need anyone to replace him, but we need a bigtime scorer. I don't care if he's playing center or whatever. We need a potent player to come back into our franchise."

Krause never was able to swing a deal. Yet the Bulls continued to win. They were less consistent during the second half of the season but managed to finish with a record of 55-27, only two victories behind the previous year's total. Scottie had the best year of his pro career, averaging 22 points, 8.7 rebounds, 5.6 assists, and 2.93 steals per game. He was the only NBA player to average more than 20 points, 8 rebounds and 5 assists per game.

But, as Jordan found out, the spotlight is bright enough to show every flaw.

During the season Pippen had his share of problems. He got himself in trouble with the Chicago fans early in the season when he gave them an obscene gesture after they had booed him. Later, he said he felt he was being booed because he was black. He apologized for the remark the following day, saying he knew that some white players with the Bulls had been booed, too.

Still, the Bulls entered the playoffs with great confidence. They swept past Cleveland in the first round of the playoffs to earn another confrontation with the Knicks.

Chicago was a heavy underdog and lost the first two games in New York. The series switched to Chicago for Game 3 and the two teams battled on even ground until there were 1.8 seconds remaining. The Bulls had the ball and coach Jackson called time out to set up a play for the final shot.

It was at that precise moment that Scottie made the worst decision of his life.

On the Chicago bench coach Jackson was diagramming a play that would have Scottie inbound the ball to Kukoc, who would turn and take the final shot. Pippen, who envisioned himself as the team's best clutch player now that Jordan was gone, was angry at Jackson's decision.

"I'm tired of this," Pippen shouted at Jackson. Scottie refused to reenter the game. Jackson was forced to call another time out since the Bulls only had four players on the court. Once play resumed, Myers replaced Pippen in the lineup and lobbed a perfect inbounds pass to Kukoc, who spun and threw in a 20-foot shot at the buzzer to win the game, 104–102. It was the fourth time during the season that Kukoc had hit a last-second game-winning shot.

The Bulls had won but Pippen had lost all kinds of respect from his teammates, the fans, and the league in general. The media came down on him hard, calling him selfish and guilty of letting his team down.

Jackson did not discipline him, however, probably realizing that without him in the line-up the Bulls had no chance to advance in the playoffs. His teammates were forgiving, too, and Pippen responded with a strong performance the rest of the playoffs, even though the Bulls eventually lost to the Knicks in seven games.

Pippen, who finished second in the league in steals, was once again named to the league's all-defensive team and he finished third in the Most Valuable Player voting. Still, his decision to remove himself from Game 3 with the Knicks overshadowed his other accomplishments.

In the weeks that followed the season, Pippen was constantly questioned about the incident.

"I really apologize for that," Pippen said. "I am human. I'm allowed to make mistakes, and it's something I've put behind me right now. I've asked the fans to forgive me for that, and hopefully I can go on with my life."

Later that year Scottie, in a first-person article for *USA Today*, explained his decision not to play the last 1.8 seconds of the Knicks game.

"It's not that I didn't want to play," he said. "I just didn't want to take the ball out of bounds. It was my competitiveness, not selfishness. I didn't feel I had to take the last shot. But the entire series was on the line at the time, and I felt that I had to at least be on the court and not standing out of bounds.

"I don't expect people to understand. It does matter, however, what people think. I might hear about it the rest of my life, but I got my point across."

What had upset Scottie was that on the previous play prior to the timeout, Kukoc had failed to clear his man out and Pippen was forced to take a jumper that didn't hit the rim before the 24-second clock expired. Now Jackson was asking Pippen to inbound the ball to Kukoc.

"People only got to see what they saw," Pippen said. "They don't see what goes on on the bench or what went on the previous play before that, which really made the whole incident happen.

"The only thing that I wanted from that last play was some respect. And I wasn't given any

Pippen shows off his MVP trophy from the 1994 All-Star Game.

respect by taking the ball out of bounds."

The Bulls' front office, though, was intent on trading Pippen during the off-season. They almost had a trade made with Seattle but SuperSonics owner Barry Ackerly nixed the deal on draft day after hearing Seattle fans didn't like it. They tried again with the Washington Bullets but that deal fell through, too.

Meanwhile, the Bulls' roster was changing. Bill Cartwright left via free agency and Paxson retired. In fact, of the nine players who played on all three championship teams, only Pippen, Armstrong, and backup center Will Perdue remained.

Pippen was upset at the team for letting his close friend, Grant, escape to Orlando. He also became angry with Bulls' management when Kukoc was signed to a six-year, $26 million contract. That made Kukoc the highest-paid Bull ever. It was more than Jordan ever made and considerably more than Pippen was making.

"I felt it was an insult to give a player that type of money who hadn't proven anything," said Pippen, "who hadn't shown that he had the right habits and mentality to come out and want to the best in the game."

When no trade transpired, Pippen showed up at training camp and saw almost a completely different team. It was clear that Pippen was going to have to be even more of a leader than he was the previous year.

"I'm out there not just playing, but trying to be like a coach and helping the new guys do things right," Pippen said.

Although Pippen played well, the Bulls hovered at the .500 mark for most of the season. Then, in the middle of March, only a month before the start of the NBA playoffs, the Bulls received the startling news that Michael Jordan was returning to basketball.

A major league baseball strike, which had wiped out the last six weeks of the 1994 season and canceled the World Series, was still ongoing during spring training. Minor leaguers had been asked by the Players Association not to cross the picket line and be branded as scabs. Jordan, who was supposed to be promoted up the Chicago White Sox chain to Triple A in 1995, wanted no part of baseball politics.

Besides, Jordan had shown he was only an ordinary baseball player at best. He had very little chance of ever making it to the major leagues, except as a curiosity piece. He longed to return to the competition of the NBA where his talent was unequaled.

In the 1995 playoffs, Chicago first faced the tough Charlotte Hornets. Alonzo Mourning, Larry Johnson, and Muggsy Bogues formed the nucleus of a team that was far stronger than the Bulls ordinarily squared off against in the first round. Chicago was able to come away the winner, but Pippen did not play well and Jordan complained that he had to carry the team by himself.

The Bulls then took on the Orlando Magic. The Magic had the best winning record in the Eastern Conference and basketball experts were predicting that the Magic were going to win a championship or three themselves, if not starting this year, then soon. The Magic featured the dynamic young duo of Shaquille O'Neal and Anfcrncc Hardaway.

The Magic won the first game. Jordan came out at the start of the second game wearing his old number 23 jersey. He had played in a number 45 jersey for all of this season, but he sensed his team needed inspiration and figured seeing "the Jordan of old" might provide that spark.

The Bulls won that game and one more. But Horace Grant, now of Orlando, helped shut Pippen down, and Chicago's postseason play was over.

Pippen had one piece of good news during the playoffs. He was named to the All-NBA team, the second time he had won the honor (and the first time in many years that Jordan had not).

Pippen was named to the All-NBA team for a third straight time at the end of the 1995-96 season, which saw the Bulls win their fourth NBA title in six years. It was a record-setting season for Chicago, which went 72-10 during the regular campaign and 15-3 during the playoffs. All told, the Bulls won more games than any team in NBA history.

Pippen was as stellar as ever, although he had learned to accept his role as basketball's best supporting player. "Michael will be remembered as the greatest player ever," Pippen said. "I just want to be remembered as a great player, period. An all-around great player."

In the 1996-97 season, Pippen was honored for his great all-around playing when he was selected to the NBA's "50 Greatest Players in NBA History." He didn't disappoint the Bulls either, starting all 82 games and leading his team in assists, steals, and three-point field goals. On February 18, 1997, Pippen scored a career high 47 points in a 134-123 win over Denver. Named NBA Player of the Week for February 24, Pippen was a logical choice for the All-Star Game. Although he was voted to the All-Defensive First Team for the sixth year in a row, Pippen dropped to the All-NBA Second Team.

The 1997-98 season began with foot surgery and Pippen was forced to sit out 35 games. He returned to the court on January 10, 1998, where his playing continues to lead the Bulls to victory.

STATISTICS

SCOTTIE PIPPEN

Year	Team	G	PPG	RPG	APG	FGM/G
1987-88	Chicago	79	7.9	3.8	2.1	3.8
1988-89	Chicago	73	14.4	6.1	3.5	5.7
1989-90	Chicago	82	16.5	6.5	5.4	6.9
1990-91	Chicago	82	17.8	7.3	6.2	7.3
1991-92	Chicago	82	21.0	7.7	7.0	8.4
1992-93	Chicago	81	18.6	7.7	6.2	7.8
1993-94	Chicago	72	22.0	8.7	5.6	8.7
1994-95	Chicago	79	21.4	8.1	5.2	8.0
1995-96	Chicago	77	19.4	6.4	5.9	7.3
1996-97	Chicago	82	20.2	6.5	5.7	7.9
1997-98	Chicago	44	19.1	5.2	5.8	7.2
1998-99	Houston	50	14.5	6.5	5.9	5.2
1999-00	Portland	82	12.5	6.3	5.0	4.7
2000-01	Portland	64	11.3	5.2	4.6	4.2
Totals		1029	16.9	6.6	5.3	7.0

NBA PLAYOFF RECORD

Year	Team	G	PPG	RPG	APG
1987-88	Chicago	10	10.0	5.2	2.4
1988-89	Chicago	17	13.1	7.6	3.9
1989-90	Chicago	15	19.3	7.2	5.5
1990-91	Chicago	17	21.6	8.9	5.8
1991-92	Chicago	22	19.5	8.8	6.7
1992-93	Chicago	19	20.1	6.9	5.6
1993-94	Chicago	10	22.8	8.3	4.6
1994-95	Chicago	11	21.1	8.1	4.8
1995-96	Chicago	18	16.9	8.5	5.9
1996-97	Chicago	19	23.3	6.8	3.8
1987-97		158	18.8	7.6	4.9

G	games	**APG**	assists per game
PPG	points per game	**FGM/G**	field goals made per game
RPG	rebounds per game		

SCOTTIE PIPPEN
A CHRONOLOGY

1965   Born to Ethel and Preston Pippen of Hamburg, Arkansas

1986   Named to the NAIA All-America team

1987   The Chicago Bulls trade for Pippen after the Seattle SuperSonics draft him with their number five pick

1990   Named to the NBA All-Star team

1991   Settles a bitter contract dispute and signs a 7-year, $24.5-million contract; he averages 17.8 points per game and helps lead the Bulls to a first-place finish in the Central Division; the Bulls beat the Los Angeles Lakers in the championship round and win their first NBA title

1992   Bulls win a second straight championship; Pippen helps lead the U.S. "Dream Team" to a gold medal at the Barcelona Olympics

1993   Again is named to the league's All-Star team and earns a spot on the league's defensive unit; steps out of Jordan's shadow and sparks the Bulls to a third consecutive NBA championship

1994   Jordan announces his retirement; Pippen becomes the team leader and has his best season, averaging 22.8 points a game; named MVP of the All-Star game

1996   Bulls win their fourth NBA championship and win more games than any team in history; Pippin and "Dream Team III" win gold medals at the Atlanta Olympics

1997   Bulls win their fifth NBA championship; Pippen leads team in assists, steals, and three-point field goals; honored as one of the "50 Greatest Players in NBA History"

1998   Makes Houston Rockets debut; named to the NBA All-Defensive First Team

1999   Signs with Portland Trailblazers; selected to NBA All-Defensive Second Team

SUGGESTIONS FOR FURTHER READING

George, Nelson. *Elevating the Game: The History and Aesthetics of Black Men in Basketball.* Simon & Schuster, 1992.

Smith, Sam. *The Jordan Rules: The Inside Story of a Turbulent Season with Michael Jordan and the Chicago Bulls.* New York: Simon & Schuster, 1992.

Stauth, Cameron. *The Golden Boys: The Unauthorized Inside Look at the U.S. Olympic Basketball Team.* New York: Pocket Books, 1992.

ABOUT THE AUTHOR

Fred McMane has been a journalist for more than 30 years. He was a writer, editor and administrator for United Press International from 1964–93, serving as the company's sports editor from 1988–93. In addition, he has served as a consultant to the Prodigy Services Company and as a copy editor for the *Newark Star-Ledger.*

Mr. McMane is the author of the following books: *The Baseball Playbook*, with Gil McDougald; *4,192: A Celebration of Pete Rose; Amazin': The Story of the 1986 New York Mets; The Worst Day I Ever Had; My Hero;* and *Winning Women.*

INDEX

PICTURE CREDITS:
AP/Wide World Photos: pp. 8, 11, 14, 31, 34, 38, 40, 43, 46, 51, 57 ; Photo by Bill Smith, courtesy Chicago Bulls, p. 2; courtesy Gursta McDonald, pp. 16, 20; courtesy University of Central Arkansas, pp. 22, 24, 26, 52; UPI/Bettmann: p. 28; Reuters/Bettmann: p. 44.